THE 10 SMARTEST ANIMALS

BY RACHEL ROSE

Minneapolis, Minnesota

Credits
Cover and title page, © F1online digitale Bildagentur GmbH/Alamy Stock Photo, © Gabriel/Adobe Stock Photos, and © jimkruger/iStock; Title Page, © F1online digitale Bildagentur GmbH/Alamy Stock Photo; 4, © Yü Lan/Adobe Stock Photos; 5, © alexlukin/Adobe Stock Photos; 6–7, © imageBROKER.com GmbH & Co. KG/Alamy Stock Photo; 8, © Arterra Picture Library/Alamy Stock Photo; 8–9, © Whittaker Wildlife/Alamy Stock Photo; 10, © Pcha988/iStock; 10–11, © Andrew Darrington/Alamy Stock Photo; 12, © Panther Media GmbH /Alamy Stock Photo; 12–13, © Arto Hakola/Alamy Stock Photo; 14–15, © Volodymyr Ivanenko/Getty Images; 15, © WhitcombeRD/iStock; 16, © elmvilla/iStock; 17, © robertharding/Alamy Stock Photo; 18, © D. R. Schrichte/Blue Planet Archive; 19, © mariusz_prusaczyk/iStock; 20–21, © Cheryl Ramalho/iStock; 22T, © webguzs/iStock; 22M, © sankai/iStock; 22B, © Badrudin/iStock; 23, © BirdImages/iStock.

Bearport Publishing Company Product Development Team
Publisher: Jen Jenson; Director of Product Development: Spencer Brinker; Managing Editor: Allison Juda; Editor: Cole Nelson; Associate Editor: Naomi Reich; Associate Editor: Tiana Tran; Art Director: Colin O'Dea; Designer: Kim Jones; Designer: Kayla Eggert; Product Development Specialist: Owen Hamlin

Statement on Usage of Generative Artificial Intelligence
Bearport Publishing remains committed to publishing high-quality nonfiction books. Therefore, we restrict the use of generative AI to ensure accuracy of all text and visual components pertaining to a book's subject. See BearportPublishing.com for details.

Library of Congress Cataloging-in-Publication Data is available at www.loc.gov or upon request from the publisher.

ISBN: 979-8-89232-641-4 (hardcover)
ISBN: 979-8-89232-690-2 (ebook)

For more information, write to Bearport Publishing, 5357 Penn Avenue South, Minneapolis, MN 55419.

CONTENTS

SMARTY-PANTS

There are millions of different **species** of animals in the world. They come in all shapes, colors, and sizes. Some are strong, some are cool, and some are cute. But there are also a lot of animals that are incredibly intelligent.

WHAT ARE THE WILD WORLD'S 10 SMARTEST ANIMALS?

Read on to decide for yourself. . . .

#10 HORSE

Neigh-ver fear, a horse is here! This four-legged friend is known for its **emotional intelligence**. A horse can easily pick up on the feelings of other creatures, including humans! It often mirrors emotions, such as acting nervous around an **anxious** rider. When a herd member is in pain, a horse might nuzzle it with its nose to provide comfort.

When in danger, their first response is to flee.

Young horses learn by watching older horses in action.

In the wild, horses work together to stay safe from predators.

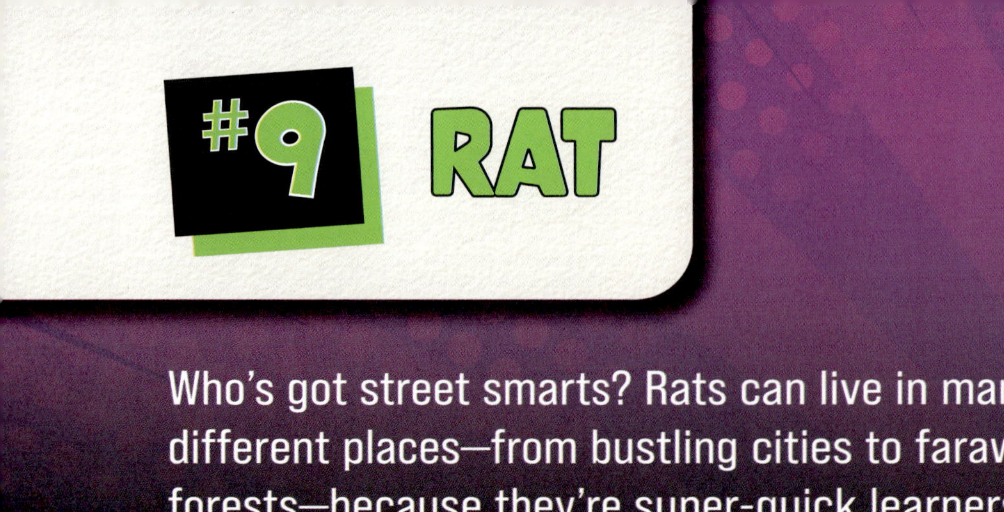

#9 RAT

Who's got street smarts? Rats can live in many different places—from bustling cities to faraway forests—because they're super-quick learners. These smarties easily **adapt** to any **environment**. In fact, the more difficult their surroundings, the smarter they become. Rats use their brains to solve problems, such as opening containers or finding their way through underground tunnels.

They are sometimes clever enough to avoid human-set traps.

These social animals share knowledge with one another.

Rats can remember good places to find food.

Whiskers help rats sense the world around them.

#8 WOLF

The hunt is on! Wolves live in large family groups called packs. Their intelligence shines when they hunt together to take down animals much bigger than themselves—and they have plenty of brainy ways of doing so. The pack often forms a circle around their prey, leaving no room for escape. Wolves also take turns chasing animals to avoid getting as tired by themselves. Now, that's teamwork!

The pack teaches and raises their young together.

Because of their hunting smarts, wolves do well in many different environments.
Howling helps lost wolves find their way back to the pack.
Wolves form lifelong friendships.

#7 ANT

They may be tiny, but scientists believe ants have the biggest brains of all insects! These smarty-ants work together in large groups called **colonies** to solve problems. For example, when they need to cross over water, some ants in the colony are quick to take action. They use their own bodies to form a bridge! Then, the others can climb over them to get to the other side. Watch your step!

They sometimes use leaves to drink drops of water.

Ants leave scent trails that lead to food so other ants know where to go.
An ant colony is made up of several thousand members.
Each ant in a colony has its own job.

#6 COMMON RAVEN

Finding food is not a problem for **resourceful** ravens. These large, smart birds can often solve problems. If mollusk shells are too hard to get to the treat inside, ravens will sometimes drop them on rocks to smash the shells open. Common ravens also search for food in garbage cans. With their sharp beaks, these clever birds can open lids and even untie knots!

Ravens sometimes dip dry bread in water to make it softer and easier for their young to eat.

These brainy birds can copy the sounds of other bird species.

Ravens often work in pairs. One digs for food, while the other keeps lookout.
They hide food from other birds to eat later.

#5 OCTOPUS

What would you do with nine brains? Ask an octopus! This smart creature has one main brain between its eyes and one in each of its eight arms. An octopus arm can move, taste, and touch without help from the main brain—making the creature an excellent multitasker. An octopus can use some arms to catch prey, while its others search for more food.

They are masters of escape, even able to get out of locked tanks!

Most octopuses can change their color and shape to **blend** in with their environments.
An octopus's main brain is shaped like a doughnut.
Octopuses collect shells and rocks to build dens.

#4 SQUIRREL

Is it a squirrel scam? When they think they're being watched by other animals, these bushy-tailed rodents have a clever way of hiding their food. The squirrels pretend to bury it. However, the animals have actually hidden the nuts and fruits under their small arms! Later, the furry creatures scurry off to bury their snacks elsewhere. Squirrels sometimes even hide their stash of food in multiple spots.

Squirrels can remember months later where they've hidden food.

To escape from predators, squirrels run in zigzags.

Squirrels sometimes shake nuts to see if they are edible.

#3 ELEPHANT

Some say elephants never forget—maybe because the animals have excellent memories! In times of dry weather, elephants can find faraway water sources they visited years before. They never forget their friends, either. Even if they haven't seen playmates since they were **calves**, elephants still remember them when they're adults.

Elephants remember long-distance **migration** routes.

Elephants sometimes use sticks as tools to scratch themselves.

They often grunt or snort to **communicate** with one another.

#2 DOLPHIN

Dolphins are some of the most intelligent animals on Earth. They use whistles, chirps, and other sounds to communicate with one another. These clever animals also use their bodies to communicate, such as when they slap their tails to warn of nearby predators. When hunting together, dolphins make clicking noises that bounce off nearby objects. Then, the sounds come back to help them find prey.

Dolphins blow bubble rings in the water to gather fish into one place.

One species of dolphins makes unique whistles. This allows the dolphins to recognize one another!
Dolphins work together in groups when they hunt.
Dolphins sometimes use shells to trap their prey.

#1 CHIMPANZEE

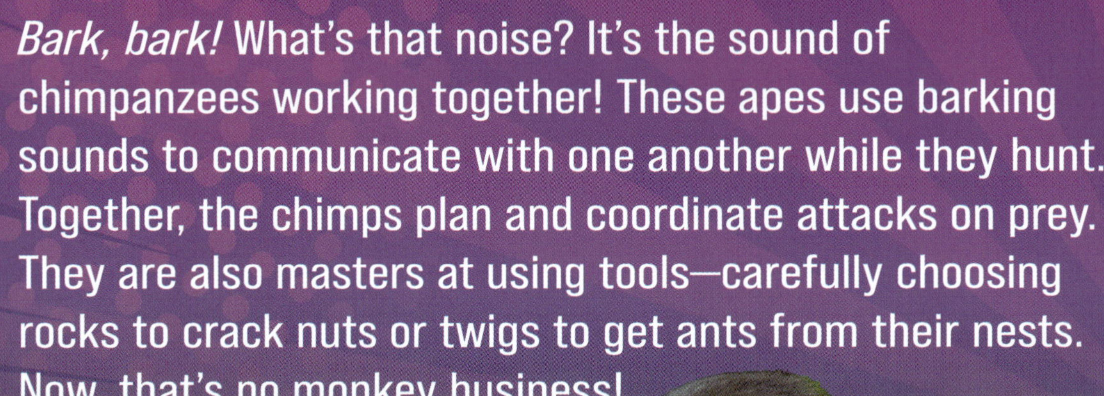

Bark, bark! What's that noise? It's the sound of chimpanzees working together! These apes use barking sounds to communicate with one another while they hunt. Together, the chimps plan and coordinate attacks on prey. They are also masters at using tools—carefully choosing rocks to crack nuts or twigs to get ants from their nests. Now, that's no monkey business!

These apes are the closest living relatives to humans.

Chimps come together in groups called **communities** or troops.

Grooming one another helps chimps bond.
Chimps are one of the few animals that can recognize themselves in mirrors.
Chimpanzees sometimes share their food with other troop members.

EVEN MORE SMART ANIMALS

These 10 animals aren't the only clever creatures in the wild. What are some other smarties that are top of the class?

HUMMINGBIRD

These tiny birds have great memories. Hummingbirds can remember every flower they visit—and they visit up to 2,000 flowers each day!

BEE

Wanna dance? Bees use moves called the waggle dance to tell other bees where the best food is.

ORANGUTAN

These great apes can be very creative. Orangutans use leaves as napkins to wipe their mouths and as hats to keep off rain.

GLOSSARY

adapt to change over time to survive in an environment or habitat

anxious worried

blend to mix in with

calves young elephants

colonies groups of ants that live together

communicate to pass information between two or more things

communities groups of chimpanzees that live together

emotional intelligence the ability to be aware of the feelings of others

environment the plants, animals, and weather of a place

migration the movement of animals from one area to another at a certain time of year

resourceful able to find quick and clever ways to solve problems

species groups that animals are divided into, according to similar characteristics

INDEX

READ MORE

Grodzicki, Jenna. *Elephant (Library of Awesome Animals).* Minneapolis: Bearport Publishing, 2022.

Temple, Colton. *Chimpanzees (Wild About Animals).* Minneapolis: Kaleidoscope, 2021.

LEARN MORE ONLINE

1. Go to **FactSurfer.com** or scan the QR code below.
2. Enter "**10 Smartest Animals**" into the search box.
3. Click on the cover of this book to see a list of websites.

ABOUT THE AUTHOR

Rachel Rose writes books for kids and teaches yoga. Her favorite animal for all time is her dog, Sandy.